It's Your Turn Snoopy

Charles M. Schulz

CORONET BOOKS
Hodder and Stoughton

First published 1975 by Fawcett Publications, Inc.
New York

Coronet edition 1978
Eleventh impression 1985

Printed and bound in Great Britain for Hodder and Stoughton Paperbacks, a division of Hodder and Stoughton Ltd., Mill Road, Dunton Green, Sevenoaks, Kent (Editorial Office: 47 Bedford Square, London, WC1 3DP) by Cox & Wyman Ltd., Reading

ISBN 0 340 22778 8

It's your turn, SNOOPY

I'LL KICK THE BALL TO YOU, AND YOU COME RUNNING DOWN THE FIELD, AND I'LL TRY TO HUG YOU
TACKLE
HUG
TACKLE
HUG
FORGET IT!
STUPID GAME!

I CAN SEE MYSELF!
I'D LOOK FUNNY WITH A BIG NOSE..
SCHULZ

IT'S SUPPERTIME!
DO YOU WANT TO GET UP, OR SHOULD I JUST SHOVE IT UNDER THE SNOW?
HA HA HA HA HA!
I HATE FUNNY WAITERS!
SCHULZ

THAT MAKES ME FEEL LIKE A STUPID BUSH!
SCHULZ

THE WORLD IS FILLED WITH COMEDIANS!
SCHULZ

*
* Merry Christmas
Schulz

WHAT A STUPID QUESTION!
WHY WOULD I FORGET THE ROOT BEER AND THE OLIVES?
SCHULZ

WOW!! I CAN'T BELIEVE IT!
WHAT A NIGHT...
THAT WOODSTOCK GIVES SOME WILD PARTIES!
SCHULZ

HERE..IT LOOKS LIKE YOU GOT A BILL FROM WOODSTOCK
A BILL? FOR WHAT?
"YOU OWE ME SIX DOLLARS FOR THE THINGS YOU BROKE AT MY NEW YEAR'S PARTY... PLEASE PAY AT ONCE!"
THAT STUPID BIRD! HIS WHOLE NEST ISN'T WORTH SIX DOLLARS! I WON'T PAY!
BESIDES, HE SERVED VERY CHEAP ROOT BEER
SCHULZ

WHAT'S THIS, ANOTHER BILL FROM WOODSTOCK?
"THIS IS YOUR SECOND NOTICE.. YOU OWE ME SIX DOLLARS FOR WHAT YOU BROKE AT MY NEW YEAR'S PARTY!"
"DON'T TRY TO GET OUT OF PAYING, BANANA NOSE!"
BANANA NOSE?
SCHULZ

POKE!

FRIENDSHIPS ARE TOO IMPORTANT TO SPOIL BY BICKERING..
TRUE
I THINK YOU AND WOODSTOCK SHOULD TRY TO TALK THINGS OUT...
HA! I CAN HEAR HIM NOW...
I SEE WHAT YOU MEAN
THANK YOU
SCHULZ

"THIS IS YOUR THIRD NOTICE! YOU OWE ME SIX DOLLARS FOR WHAT YOU BROKE AT MY NEW YEAR'S PARTY!"
SO PAY UP!!
MEOW!
CATS HAVE THE RIGHT IDEA!
SCHULZ

WHAT DO YOU DO WITH TWO FRIENDS WHO ARE HAVING A MISUNDERSTANDING?
STRAIGHTEN THEM OUT! SHOW 'EM WHERE THEY'VE GONE WRONG!! TELL 'EM TO SHAPE UP!!!
IS THAT GOOD PSYCHOLOGY?
IN STRICT MEDICAL TERMS, IT'S CALLED "BUTTING IN"!
SCHULZ

I HAVE A SUGGESTION
DOESN'T EVERYONE?
WHY DON'T YOU TRY TO FIND OUT WHAT IT WAS THAT YOU BROKE AT WOODSTOCK'S PARTY?
MAYBE THAT WOULD BE THE FIRST STEP TOWARD YOUR RECONCILIATION..
I ALWAYS TRIP ON THAT FIRST STEP
SCHULZ

DO I HEAR THE FLUTTER OF WINGS?
RATS! IT'S ONLY A LEAF! I THOUGHT IT MIGHT BE WOODSTOCK..
MAYBE I SHOULD WALK OVER TO SEE HIM...MAYBE WE CAN HAVE A LITTLE TALK, AND GET THINGS SETTLED....I'LL DO IT!!

WOODSTOCK! THAT WAS WOODSTOCK WHO JUST FLEW OVER!
HE WAS GOING TO SEE ME, AND I WAS GOING TO SEE HIM!
BONK!
EVEN ON A CLEAR DAY, WOODSTOCK FLIES IN A FOG!
SCHULZ

WE'LL GO OVER TO MY HOUSE...
WE'LL QUAFF A FEW ROOT BEERS, AND WE'LL SETTLE OUR DIFFERENCES LIKE CIVILIZED GENTLEMEN...
GULP GULP GULP
QUAFF QUAFF QUAFF
IT NEVER FAILS...THREE ROOT BEERS AND WOODSTOCK FALLS SOUND ASLEEP!
Z
SCHULZ

"I INVITED YOU TO MY NEW YEAR'S PARTY BECAUSE YOU ARE MY FRIEND"
"THERE WAS SOMEONE ELSE AT THE PARTY THAT I WANTED YOU TO MEET"
"SHE'S THE CUTEST LITTLE BIRD I'VE EVER KNOWN, AND YOU MONOPOLIZED HER THE WHOLE EVENING.."
"IT BROKE MY HEART.....THAT'S WHY I SENT YOU A BILL FOR SIX DOLLARS.."
SCHULZ

I SPOILED WOODSTOCK'S PARTY!
HE HAD INVITED THIS CUTE LITTLE BIRD THAT HE'S IN LOVE WITH, BUT HE NEVER GOT TO TALK WITH HER BECAUSE I TALKED WITH HER THE WHOLE EVENING!
SO HE SENT ME A BILL FOR SIX DOLLARS FOR A BROKEN HEART! OH, WOODSTOCK, MY LITTLE FRIEND OF FRIENDS...
DON'T YOU REALIZE THAT YOUR HEART IS WORTH MUCH MUCH MORE THAN SIX DOLLARS?!!
SIGH
SCHULZ

IT HAS BEEN FORTY-FIVE MINUTES SINCE I FIRST CAME INTO SCHOOL THIS MORNING...
I FIND, UNFORTUNATELY, THAT I AM NOT ANY SMARTER NOW THAN WHEN I ARRIVED....IF IT IS TRUE THAT NATURE ABHORS A VACUUM, I MAY EVEN BE A LITTLE DUMBER!! NOW, THEREFORE, I WOULD LIKE TO...
YES, MA'AM?
RATS! I HAD A PRETTY GOOD SPEECH GOING THERE FOR A MINUTE!
SCHULZ

THE OLDEN DAYS WERE BETTER..
IN THE OLDEN DAYS, MEN USED TO WALK BY WITH TALL BLACK HATS ON, AND KIDS USED TO THROW SNOWBALLS AT THEM
BAD SHOW, LADS!
SCHULZ

IF WE WERE MARRIED, I'D BE REAL NICE TO YOU
I'D ALWAYS GET UP IN THE MORNING BEFORE YOU
WHAT FOR?
TO FRY YOUR COFFEE!
SCHULZ

IF I COULD ORDER YOU TO SEND ME FLOWERS, WOULD YOU DO IT?
NO, I'D GO TO JAIL FIRST
I'D COME TO VISIT YOU!

WHAT HAPPENS IF YOU PRACTICE FOR TWENTY YEARS, AND THEN END UP NOT BEING RICH AND FAMOUS?
THE JOY IS IN THE PLAYING
YOU'RE KIDDING!
SCHULZ

WOODSTOCK'S NEST
NEXT NINE EXITS
SCHULZ

HANG ON!
HERE WE GO!

WHEE!
OH, NO! I CAN'T BELIEVE IT!
WOODSTOCK HAS LOST HIS RETAINER!
SCHULZ

STAY!
GO BACK! STAY!

GO BACK!
BACK, I SAY! BACK!
SIGH SOME KIDS HAVE DOGS WHO TRY TO FOLLOW THEM TO SCHOOL...
SCHULZ

I'VE BEEN THINKING ABOUT SOMETHING..
CHARLIE BROWN HAS REALLY BEEN A DEDICATED BASEBALL MANAGER..HE'S DEDICATED HIS WHOLE LIFE TO OUR TEAM....
THEREFORE, I THINK THAT WE SHOULD GIVE HIM A TESTIMONIAL DINNER!
DO YOU THINK HE REALLY DESERVES A WHOLE DINNER?
HOW ABOUT A TESTIMONIAL SNACK?
SCHULZ

HI, VIOLET
HELLO, LINUS
I'M TRYING TO ORGANIZE A TESTIMONIAL DINNER FOR CHARLIE BROWN...
WOULD YOU BE INTERESTED IN COMING ?
WHAT'S ON TV THAT NIGHT?

YOU KNOW WHAT?
IF WE'RE GOING TO HAVE A TESTIMONIAL DINNER FOR CHARLIE BROWN, IT SHOULD BE A SURPRISE...
THAT'S RIGHT...HE SHOULDN'T KNOW ABOUT IT...
LET'S NOT EVEN INVITE HIM!

HELLO, PEPPERMINT PATTY? WE'RE THINKING ABOUT HAVING A TESTIMONIAL DINNER FOR CHARLIE BROWN.. COULD YOU COME?
WHAT HAPPENS AT A TESTIMONIAL DINNER?
WELL, EVERYONE GETS UP, AND SAYS ALL SORTS OF THINGS ABOUT WHAT A GREAT PERSON THE GUEST OF HONOR IS...
IT'S GOING TO BE A QUIET EVENING!
SCHULZ

Dear Joe Shlabotnik,
How would you like to be our Master of Ceremonies?
We are having a testimonial dinner for our manager who is also your number-one fan.
WON'T IT BE GREAT IF HE CAN COME? JOE SHLABOTNIK IS CHARLIE BROWN'S FAVORITE BASEBALL PLAYER...
HE PROBABLY WON'T BE ABLE TO GET AWAY...THEY'RE PRETTY BUSY DOWN AT THE CAR WASH!
SCHULZ

IT'S GOING TO BE A TESTIMONIAL DINNER FOR CHARLIE BROWN
I KNOW HIM... THE ROUND-HEADED KID..
IT'S TO SHOW OUR APPRECIATION FOR ALL HE'S DONE AS OUR TEAM MANAGER
I HATE SHOWING APPRECIATION
ANYWAY, YOU'RE INVITED SO PLEASE TRY TO COME..
I WON'T GO UNLESS I CAN SIT AT THE HEAD TABLE!
SCHULZ

LOOK! I RECEIVED AN ANSWER FROM JOE SHLABOTNIK!
"DEAR FRIENDS, I ACCEPT YOUR INVITATION TO ATTEND THE TESTIMONIAL DINNER FOR MR. BROWN.. MY USUAL FEE FOR SUCH AFFAIRS IS ONE HUNDRED DOLLARS"
ONE HUNDRED DOLLARS?!! TELL HIM THAT ALL WE CAN AFFORD IS FIFTY CENTS..
"P.S. I'LL TAKE IT!"
SCHULZ

HOW ARE PLANS GOING FOR THE BIG TESTIMONIAL DINNER, LINUS?
GREAT! HAVE YOU EVER HEARD OF JOE SHLABOTNIK? HE WAS LAST-ROUND DRAFT CHOICE IN THE GREEN GRASS LEAGUE...
HE'S GOING TO BE OUR GUEST SPEAKER
HOW APPROPRIATE!

ALL RIGHT, GIRLS, LET'S SETTLE DOWN!
THE MEETING WILL COME TO ORDER!
AS MEMBERS OF THE FOOD COMMITTEE, WE HAVE TO DECIDE WHAT TO SERVE AT CHARLIE BROWN'S TESTIMONIAL DINNER...
IS THERE SUCH A THING AS A LOSER'S SALAD?
SCHULZ

OKAY, MARCIE, YOU AND I ARE THE INVITATION COMMITTEE
NOW, HERE'S A LIST OF ALL THE PEOPLE WHO ARE TO RECEIVE INVITATIONS TO CHARLIE BROWN'S TESTIMONIAL DINNER.... AT THE BOTTOM OF EACH ONE, WE PUT R.S.V.P.
WHAT DOES R.S.V.P. MEAN, SIR?
"REVISED STANDARD VERSION, PLEASE"
I NEVER UNDERSTAND YOUR JOKES, SIR...
STOP CALLING ME "SIR"!
SCHULZ

WE'VE ADDRESSED A LOT OF INVITATIONS, HAVEN'T WE, SIR?
I THINK I'M GETTING SICK FROM LICKING ALL THESE STAMPS AND ENVELOPES
BY GOLLY, THAT STUPID CHUCK BETTER APPRECIATE ALL THE WORK WE'RE DOING TO GIVE HIM THIS TESTIMONIAL DINNER..BESIDES, HE'S A TERRIBLE BALL PLAYER...
IF WE DON'T BELIEVE IN WHAT WE'RE DOING, AREN'T WE BEING HYPOCRITICAL, SIR?
I HATE QUESTIONS LIKE THAT!
SCHULZ

THERE'S STILL QUITE A BIT OF WORK TO DO ON THE TESTIMONIAL DINNER...
I WAS WONDERING IF YOU'D CARE TO SERVE ON THE FLOWER COMMITTEE...
SO MUCH FOR THE FLOWER COMMITTEE!
SCHULZ

HELLO, CHUCK? AS CHAIRWOMAN OF THE INVITATION COMMITTEE, I HAVE A SURPRISE FOR YOU!
I COULDN'T TELL YOU BEFORE BECAUSE THIS HAS ALL BEEN VERY HUSH-HUSH, BUT NOW I CAN TELL YOU...GUESS WHAT...WE'RE GOING TO GIVE YOU A TESTIMONIAL DINNER!!
HOW DOES THAT HIT YOU, CHUCK? ARE YOU EXCITED? ARE YOU SMILING, CHUCK?
I'M SMILING!!!
SCHULZ

WHAT'S THE MATTER WITH YOU, BIG BROTHER?
YOU LOOK LIKE YOU JUST SWALLOWED A CHOCOLATE CAKE...
THEY'RE GOING TO GIVE ME A TESTIMONIAL DINNER!
ALL THE KIDS THAT I PLAY BASEBALL WITH ARE GOING TO GIVE ME A TESTIMONIAL DINNER!
CHECK THE CALENDAR...IT MUST BE APRIL FOOL'S DAY!
SCHULZ

THIS IS GOING TO BE A GREAT EVENING, MARCIE! OL' CHUCK IS REALLY GOING TO BE EXCITED!
I'M NOT GOING, SIR
YOU'RE WHAT?!
YOU KNOW WE'RE ALL JUST BEING HYPOCRITES, SIR...YOU KNOW THAT WE DON'T REALLY THINK CHUCK DESERVES A TESTIMONIAL DINNER!
I CAN'T GO THROUGH WITH IT! I'M GOING HOME!
AAUGH!!
SCHULZ

WHAT'S ALL THE YELLING ABOUT?
THIS STUPID MARCIE SAYS WE'RE ALL HYPOCRITES!
SHE SAYS WE DON'T REALLY BELIEVE THAT CHUCK IS A GOOD BASEBALL MANAGER SO OUR WHOLE DINNER IS HYPOCRITICAL!
I'M NOT STUPID, SIR
BY GOLLY, IF IT WEREN'T FOR ONE THING, I'D SLUG HER!!
WHAT'S THAT?
DEEP DOWN, I KNOW SHE'S RIGHT!
OH, GOOD GRIEF!!
SCHULZ

WELCO
CANCEL THE DINNER?
WE CAN'T CANCEL THE DINNER!! EVERYONE IS ALREADY HERE! EVERYONE IS ALREADY SEATED! EVEN THE GUEST OF HONOR IS HERE!!
IT'S ALL HYPOCRITICAL ...WE'RE NOT REALLY SINCERE ..WE'RE ALL GOING TO SAY THINGS ABOUT CHARLIE BROWN THAT WE DON'T REALLY BELIEVE, AND IT'S ALL HYPOCRITICAL!
I WOULD HAVE ENJOYED EVEN A HYPOCRITICAL DINNER
SCHULZ

WHO IN THE WORLD COULD BE CALLING AT THREE O'CLOCK IN THE MORNING?
WHO? NO, THE DINNER WAS CANCELED...WELL, IT'S A LONG STORY...
YES, WE WERE WONDERING WHAT HAD HAPPENED TO YOU... I'M SORRY YOU GOT LOST...ALL RIGHT... MAYBE NEXT TIME...
GOOD NIGHT, MR. SHLABOTNIK

NOW SHOWING
"Life Goes On!"
DO YOU THINK THAT THINGS CHANGE AS WE GET OLDER, CHUCK ?
WELL, MY DAD HAS TOLD ME ABOUT THIS VERY NICE THEATER THAT USED TO BE IN THE NEIGHBORHOOD WHERE HE GREW UP...

WHEN HE WAS VERY SMALL, THE THEATER SEEMED HUGE, BUT AS THE YEARS WENT BY, THE THEATER GOT NARROWER AND NARROWER...
NARROWER AND NARROWER? HOW COULD A THEATER GET NARROWER AND NARROWER?
ARE YOU GETTING PHILOSOPHICAL ON ME, CHUCK?
MAYBE THERE COMES A TIME, WHEN YOU GET EVEN OLDER, WHEN THE THEATER BECOMES WIDE AGAIN...
GIRLS DON'T LIKE IT WHEN A BOY GETS PHILOSOPHICAL, CHUCK
I'M GOING HOME...I HAVE A FEELING THAT OUR BACK YARD IS SHRINKING...
SCHULZ

BOOT!

WELL, PERHAPS I CAN.. CLEAR UP A LITTLE MISCONCEPTION FOR YOU
SNOWSTORMS ARE NOT CAUSED BY KICKING A SNOWMAN!
WHEW
SIGH
SCHULZ

DID YOU HAVE A GOOD TIME SKIING?
I HAD A GREAT TIME
I ONLY BROKE FOUR LEGS...
FORTUNATELY, THEY WERE ALL ON OTHER PEOPLE!
SCHULZ

YOU KNOW WHAT?
YESTERDAY I WAS ALMOST HAPPY...
FOR ONE BRIEF MOMENT I THOUGHT I WAS WINNING IN THE GAME OF LIFE...
BUT THERE WAS A FLAG ON THE PLAY!
SCHULZ

SURPRISE!
WHAT'S THIS?
FRENCH TOAST! I MADE IT MYSELF
BLEAH!! IT TASTES AWFUL!
REALLY?
MAYBE I SHOULDN'T HAVE MADE IT WITH CHOCOLATE MILK...
SCHULZ

"A PINCH-HITTER MAY BE DESIGNATED TO BAT FOR THE STARTING PITCHER AND ALL SUBSEQUENT PITCHERS IN ANY GAME WITHOUT OTHERWISE AFFECTING THE STATUS OF THE PITCHERS IN THE GAME.."
" FAILURE TO DESIGNATE A PINCH-HITTER PRIOR TO THE GAME PRECLUDES THE USE OF A DESIGNATED PINCH-HITTER FOR THE GAME... PINCH-HITTERS FOR A DESIGNATED PINCH-HITTER MAY BE USED..."
"ANY SUBSTITUTE PINCH-HITTER FOR A DESIGNATED PINCH-HITTER HIMSELF BECOMES A DESIGNATED PINCH-HITTER .. A REPLACED DESIGNATED PINCH-HITTER SHALL NOT RE-ENTER THE GAME "
I PROBABLY WON'T GET TO BAT THE WHOLE SEASON...
SCHULZ

!
I FIND IT DIFFICULT TO BELIEVE THAT HE WAS CALLED TO THE WHITE COURTESY TELEPHONE!
SCHULZ

FORGET IT!
SCHULZ

5:48
AHEM!
IT'S NOT SIX O'CLOCK YET! I REFUSE TO FEED YOU EVEN ONE MINUTE BEFORE SIX O'CLOCK!
I KNOW YOU! I'M ON TO YOUR LITTLE GAME!

TODAY YOU WANT TO BE FED AT FIVE O'CLOCK... TOMORROW IT WOULD BE FOUR O'CLOCK..THE NEXT DAY IT WOULD BE THREE O'CLOCK..
PRETTY SOON YOU'D HAVE WORKED YOUR WAY BACK AROUND THE CLOCK, AND YOU'D HAVE PICKED UP AN EXTRA SUPPER!
WELL, YOU CAN JUST FORGET IT!
HE'S SMARTER THAN I THOUGHT HE WAS!
SCHULZ

HERE, YOU GOT AN OFFICIAL LETTER..
OOO! I LOVE OFFICIAL LETTERS!
AT LEAST YOU KNOW THAT IT'S NOT A TRAFFIC CITATION..
DOGS NEVER GET TRAFFIC CITATIONS NOR JURY DUTY.
THAT'S WHAT IS KNOWN AS "SMALL CONSOLATION"!
SCHULZ

Dear Dog, This is to inform you that you are one of the finalists for this year's Daisy Hill Puppy Cup Award.
THE DAISY HILL PUPPY CUP!! I'VE BEEN NOMINATED FOR THE DAISY HILL PUPPY CUP!!!
WHEEEEEEE!
STUPID BEAGLE!
SCHULZ

"TO BE ELIGIBLE FOR THE DAISY HILL PUPPY CUP, NOMINEE MUST FILL OUT THE ENCLOSED FORM"
Name of Owner
?
CHARLIE BROWN!!!
HOW EMBARRASSING..
SCHULZ

SO THE DAISY HILL PUPPY CUP IS AWARDED TO THE OUTSTANDING NEIGHBORHOOD DOG OF THE YEAR..
YOU'RE GOING TO HAVE SOME PRETTY STRONG COMPETITION
WHAT MAKES YOU THINK YOU CAN WIN?
I'M SO CUTE!
SCHULZ

HERE ARE SOME MORE RULES ABOUT THE DAISY HILL PUPPY CUP AWARD
"EACH NOMINEE MUST SUBMIT FIVE LETTERS FROM INTERESTED PARTIES STATING WHY HE SHOULD BE NAMED 'THE NEIGHBORHOOD DOG OF THE YEAR' "
DON'T ASK ME TO WRITE A LETTER FOR YOU! I WOULDN'T RECOMMEND YOU FOR "DOG OF THE MINUTE"!
WHAAH!
AND CRYING WON'T HELP!!
SCHULZ

I would like to recommend my dog for the Daisy Hill Puppy Cup.
He is brave and loyal and
SNAP SNAP
impatient

YOU WANT ME TO WRITE A LETTER RECOMMENDING YOU FOR 'NEIGHBORHOOD DOG OF THE YEAR'?
I CAN'T DO IT...I DON'T THINK THAT YOU REALLY ARE TYPICAL OF A NEIGHBORHOOD DOG...
ZIP!
THIS IS BLACKMAIL!!
SCHULZ

I would like to recommend Snoopy for Neighborhood Dog of the Year.
He is truly a dog among dogs.
HOW'S THAT?
GREAT!
WHAT A WAY TO GET YOUR BLANKET BACK!
WHAT A WAY TO GET A LETTER OF RECOMMENDATION!
SCHULZ

LET'S SEE NOW...I HAVE TWO LETTERS OF RECOMMENDATION
I.. HAVE ONE FROM THAT ROUND-HEADED KID AND ONE FROM THAT STUPID KID WITH THE BLANKET... I NEED THREE MORE..
FORGET IT!
SIGH
SCHULZ

YOU WANT ME TO WRITE A LETTER RECOMMENDING YOU FOR 'NEIGHBORHOOD DOG OF THE YEAR'?
WHEN DID YOU EVER SAY ANYTHING NICE ABOUT BEETHOVEN?
I NEVER KNEW THAT BEETHOVEN WANTED TO BE 'NEIGHBORHOOD DOG OF THE YEAR'
SCHULZ

I would like to nominate Snoopy for Neighborhood Dog of the Year because
he's kind of fuzzy.
SCHULZ

He is truly a good dog.
type type type
He is also a loyal friend.
Therefore, I would like to recommend ol' banana nose for Neighborhood Dog of the Year.
HEE HEE HEE HEE HEE HEE
SCHULZ

I THINK THEY'RE GOING TO ANNOUNCE THE WINNER OF THE DAISY HILL PUPPY CUP TOMORROW
DOES SNOOPY THINK HE HAS A CHANCE? IS HE CONFIDENT?
OH, YES... HE'S VERY CONFIDENT...
WHY ELSE WOULD HE BE BUILDING A TROPHY CASE?
SCHULZ

IT'S IN THE PAPER!!!
THEY'VE ANNOUNCED THE WINNER OF THE "DAISY HILL PUPPY CUP"!
I THINK I'M GOING TO FAINT..
DON'T FAINT!
KLUNK!!
DIDN'T YOU HEAR ME?
QUIET PLEASE! NEVER INTERRUPT A GOOD FAINT!
SCHULZ

THEY'VE ANNOUNCED THE WINNER...
DID I WIN? DID I WIN? TELL ME I WON! DID I WIN?
YOU DIDN'T WIN!
AAUGH!
I HATE THE WORLD! I HATE EVERYBODY AND EVERYTHING IN THE WHOLE STUPID WORLD-WIDE WORLD!!
THERE'S NOTHING LIKE A GOOD LOSER
SCHULZ

WHEN YOU'VE LOST AT SOMETHING, YOU CAN REACT IN TWO WAYS...
ONE WAY IS TO ANALYZE JUST WHY YOU LOST...TRY TO FIGURE OUT WHAT YOUR WEAKNESSES WERE, AND THEN TRY TO IMPROVE SO THAT NEXT TIME YOU CAN WIN..
BLEAH!
THAT'S THE OTHER WAY!

I CAN'T BELIEVE IT!
YOU'RE GOING TO STOP EATING JUST BECAUSE YOU DIDN'T WIN THE DAISY HILL PUPPY CUP?
DOES YOUR STOMACH KNOW ABOUT THIS?
WE'VE TALKED IT OVER
YOUR STOMACH MUST BE VERY UNDERSTANDING
WE HAVE WHAT IS KNOWN AS A CLOSE RELATIONSHIP
SCHULZ

BAM! BAM! BAM!
YOUR HUNGER STRIKE DIDN'T LAST VERY LONG, DID IT?
I LEARNED SOMETHING..
THE BRAIN MAY BE IMPORTANT..
..BUT THE STOMACH IS STILL IN CHARGE!
SCHULZ

PAT
PAT
PAT
WHAT IN THE WORLD ARE YOU DOING?
PAT
PAT
PATTING BIRDS ON THE HEAD... I HAVE FOUND THAT WHENEVER I GET REALLY DEPRESSED, PATTING BIRDS ON THE HEAD CHEERS ME UP...

THE BIRDS ALSO SEEM TO LIKE IT
SIGH
THERE ARE OTHER WAYS TO CURE DEPRESSION...YOU DON'T HAVE TO PAT BIRDS ON THE HEAD!
SO CUT IT OUT!!
!
!
boot
SCHULZ

CRUNCH
YOU KNOW WHAT MAKES KIND OF A GOOD HOBBY? SAVING STRING!
SCHULZ

I DID IT!
I'M IN THE ALPHA STATE!
SCHULZ

MOST BIRDS LAND BETWEEN THE LITTLE POINTY THINGS...
SCHULZ

YOU JUST THINK YOU'RE CUTE BECAUSE YOU'RE CUTE!
SCHULZ

YOU KNOW WHAT?
WHEN I'M WITH YOU, I'M SO HAPPY THAT I'M AFRAID MY HEART IS GOING TO POP
DON'T WORRY ABOUT IT..
NO ONE HAS EVER DIED OF "HEART POP"!
SCHULZ

MAIL
OH, NO!
I KNEW THIS WAS GOING TO HAPPEN SOMETIME...
MY BLANKET HAS BEEN RECALLED!
SCHULZ

He was a very rich cowboy..
He had a car and a horse..
He kept his car in the carport....
And he kept his horse in the horseport.
SCHULZ

April 1
A NEW MONTH AGAIN..
TODAY IS APRIL FOOL'S DAY, CHARLIE BROWN..
I THINK I'LL PLAY A LITTLE JOKE ON YOU...I THINK I'LL TRY A LITTLE TRICK...
YOU UNDERSTAND WHAT I'M SAYING, DON'T YOU? YOU UNDERSTAND THAT THIS IS APRIL FOOL'S DAY? YOU'RE SURE? I WANT TO BE CERTAIN THAT YOU UNDERSTAND! OKAY?

HEY, CHARLIE BROWN, GUESS WHAT! THAT LITTLE RED-HAIRED GIRL IS OUTSIDE, AND SHE WANTS TO GIVE YOU A HUG AND A KISS!!
REALLY?
WOW! THIS IS FANTASTIC!
APRIL FOOL!
JUST LIKE SHOOTING FISH IN A BARREL!
SCHULZ

POWER TO MY KIND!
THIS IS THE MOMENT I WAIT FOR ALL WINTER LONG...
IT'S A STRANGE FEELING WHEN YOU WALK UP ONTO THE MOUND FOR THE FIRST TIME EACH SPRING..
SORT OF GIVES YOU A FEELING OF POWER, EH, CHARLIE BROWN?
OH, NO, IT'S MORE A FEELING OF... WELL, IT'S KIND OF HARD TO DESCRIBE..
I'D THINK IT WOULD BE A FEELING OF POWER..

NO, I THINK IT'S MORE A FEELING OF NEWNESS...AFTER ALL, IT'S A NEW SEASON AND A NEW BALL GAME...IT'S THAT KIND OF FEELING..
NOT POWER?
IT'S ALSO A FEELING OF BEING PART OF A GREAT TRADITION
I SHOULD THINK THERE'D BE SORT OF A FEELING OF POWER
I THINK IT'S SOMETHING THAT HAS TO BE EXPERIENCED
LET ME TRY...WILL YOU LET ME TRY?
OH, YES, CHARLIE BROWN... I SEE WHAT YOU MEAN!
IT GIVES YOU A FEELING OF POWER!
SIGH
SCHULZ

POW!

C'MON, RERUN, I'M GOING TO TAKE YOU FOR A LITTLE WALK..
IT'S ABOUT TIME YOU GOT A LOOK AT THE OUTSIDE WORLD
WELL, WHAT DO YOU THINK?
YOU MEAN THIS IS IT?
SCHULZ

HI, NEW KID!
SLURP!
BLEAH!
HOW CAN YOU TELL SOMEONE THAT HE TASTES TERRIBLE?
SCHULZ

THINGS SURE AREN'T THE WAY I EXPECTED THEM TO BE..
WHEN I WAS FIRST BORN, EVERYONE FLOCKED AROUND, BUT NOW I NEVER SEE ANYONE! PEOPLE SEEMED TO LAUGH A LOT MORE IN THOSE DAYS, TOO...
SIGH
ONLY A YEAR OLD, AND ALREADY I'M LIVING IN THE PAST!

CHARLIE BROWN, THIS IS MY BROTHER, "RERUN"... CAN HE BE ON OUR TEAM?
..A LITTLE KID LIKE THAT?
HOW CAN HE HELP OUR TEAM?
HE DOESN'T SMOKE!
SCHULZ

THIS IS SOME TEAM I'VE GOT THIS YEAR..
A BEAGLE AT SHORTSTOP...
A SECOND BASEMAN WITH A BLANKET...
AND A LEFT FIELDER WHO'S STILL ON THE BOTTLE!
SCHULZ

I DON'T KNOW, LUCY...
I WONDER IF A LITTLE KID LIKE "RERUN" SHOULD BE OUT IN LEFT FIELD...
A FLY BALL WOULD KILL HIM
NOT IF HE RUNS FROM IT!
SCHULZ

OKAY, RERUN, THIS IS OUR FIRST GAME OF THE SEASON
I'M GOING TO LET YOU START IN LEFT FIELD AS A FAVOR TO YOUR SISTER...
JUST DO THE BEST YOU CAN, AND TRY NOT TO GET KILLED BY A FLY BALL!
WHAT ARE WE PLAYING FOR, THE STANLEY CUP?
SCHULZ

HEY, MANAGER, MY GLOVE IS SO STIFF I CAN'T CATCH THE BALL!
THAT'S BECAUSE YOU HAVEN'T USED IT ALL WINTER...TRY RUBBING A LITTLE NEAT'S-FOOT OIL INTO IT
FORGET IT!
I HATE ANY SPORT WHERE YOU HAVE TO TAKE CARE OF YOUR EQUIPMENT!
SCHULZ

DO YOU REALIZE THAT WE HAVE THE LOSINGEST TEAM IN THE HISTORY OF BASEBALL?
I REFUSE TO ACCEPT THAT!
UNFORTUNATELY, YOUR REFUSAL DOES NOT ALTER THE FACT
I REFUSE TO ACCEPT THAT ALSO!
UNFORTUNATELY, YOUR REFUSAL ALSO TO ACCEPT THE FACT THAT YOUR REFUSAL DOES NOT ALTER THE FACT ALSO DOES NOT ALTER THE FACT OF OUR BEING THE LOSINGEST
I'LL ACCEPT THAT!
SCHULZ

HEY, MANAGER, DO YOU THINK THIS GAME WILL BE OVER BY DARK?
I HOPE SO....WHY?
I HAVE NO DESIRE TO BE CHOMPED BY A NIGHT SNAKE!
A NIGHT SNAKE?
ONCE YOU GET CHOMPED BY A NIGHT SNAKE, YOU'VE HAD IT!
SCHULZ

HEY, MANAGER, I WAS JUST WONDERING IF...
THIS IS RIDICULOUS!! HOW CAN I PITCH A BALL GAME WITH PEOPLE COMING UP TO ME ALL THE TIME WITH QUESTIONS?
YOU NEED A SECRETARY, CHARLIE BROWN... YOU NEED SOMEONE TO SCREEN YOUR CALLERS...
I'M SORRY...OUR MANAGER CAN'T SEE YOU NOW...HE'S BUSY PITCHING!
I CAN'T STAND IT...
SCHULZ

RERUN IS UP AGAIN!
CHARLIE BROWN, DO YOU REALIZE WE'RE ABOUT TO WIN OUR FIRST GAME OF THE SEASON?
IF RERUN GETS ANOTHER WALK, WE WIN!
HE'S SO LITTLE THEY CAN'T PITCH TO HIM!!
BALL THREE
EVERYBODY'S YELLING AND SCREAMING... WE MUST BE WINNING THE STANLEY CUP!

BALL FOUR!
WE WON! WE WON, CHARLIE BROWN!!
WE WON OUR FIRST GAME OF THE SEASON! WE FINALLY WON!! WE WON!! WE WON!!!
I THINK I'M GOING TO CRY..
SCHULZ

WE WON, CHARLIE BROWN! C'MON, LET'S GO HOME, AND CELEBRATE!
NO! FIRST I HAVE TO WAIT FOR THE OPPOSING MANAGER TO COME OVER AND CONGRATULATE ME
EVERY YEAR I HAVE TO START THE SEASON BY GOING OVER AND CONGRATULATING THE OTHER MANAGER FOR BEATING US...THIS YEAR HE HAS TO COME TO ME! I'M GOING TO WAIT RIGHT HERE 'TIL HE COMES OVER AND CONGRATULATES ME..
SCHULZ

WE WON OUR FIRST GAME OF THE SEASON... I CAN'T BELIEVE IT!
I WONDER HOW THE OTHER TEAM FEELS...
I DON'T KNOW...WHEN WE LOSE, I'M MISERABLE...WHEN WE WIN, I FEEL GUILTY!
SCHULZ

HEY, BIG BROTHER, THE TELEPHONE WAS FOR YOU
BUT I JUST GOT TO SLEEP...
IT WAS SOME MAN WITH A DEEP VOICE
I THINK HE SAID HE WAS THE LEAGUE PRESIDENT
THE LEAGUE PRESIDENT? WHY WOULD HE BE CALLING ME?
HEY! THE PHONE ISN'T EVEN OFF THE HOOK!
I HUNG UP ON HIM!!
SCHULZ

HELLO? IS THIS THE LEAGUE PRESIDENT? I'M SORRY WE WERE DISCONNECTED..
YOU WEREN'T DISCONNECTED.. I HUNG UP ON HIM!
YES, SIR...WE WON OUR FIRST GAME TODAY..I'M VERY HAPPY...
HE SOUNDED KIND OF PUSHY SO I HUNG UP ON HIM!
LEAGUE HEADQUARTERS? THEY WANT TO SEE ME AT LEAGUE HEADQUARTERS?
WHY DON'T YOU JUST HANG UP ON HIM?
YES, SIR..TOMORROW MORNING AT LEAGUE HEADQUARTERS...YES, SIR...GOOD NIGHT...

SO THERE I WAS, SOUND ASLEEP... SUDDENLY I GET A CALL FROM THE LEAGUE PRESIDENT..
AND HE TOLD YOU TO REPORT TODAY TO LEAGUE HEADQUARTERS? IS THAT WHERE WE'RE GOING NOW?
WE'RE HERE! THIS IS IT!
A BICYCLE REPAIR SHOP?
CLASS!
SCHULZ

YES, SIR; I'M THE TEAM MANAGER AND THIS IS OUR SECOND BASEMAN, LINUS VAN PELT..
AND YOU'RE THE LEAGUE PRESIDENT? WE'RE VERY GLAD TO KNOW YOU, SIR
YOU HAVE A VERY NICE BICYCLE REPAIR SHOP HERE
ONE OF MY GREAT REGRETS IS THAT I NEVER GOT TO MEET JUDGE KENESAW MOUNTAIN LANDIS!
SCHULZ

SOMETHING WAS WRONG WITH OUR FIRST GAME?
BUT WE WON IT, SIR! WE WON IT FAIR AND SQUARE! THAT'S THE FIRST GAME WE'VE EVER WON!
YOU SAY A GROUP OF PARENTS GOT TOGETHER? BUT WHY?!
IN ALL THIS WORLD, CHARLIE BROWN, THERE IS NOTHING MORE FRIGHTENING THAN THE GETTING TOGETHER OF A GROUP OF PARENTS!
SCHULZ

GAMBLING?
GAMBLING?
YOU'RE TAKING AWAY OUR GAME BECAUSE OF GAMBLING?
WHO IN THE WORLD WOULD EVER BET ON OUR TEAM?!!!
SCHULZ

A GAMBLING SCANDAL! I'M DISGRACED!!
WE HAVE TO FORFEIT THE ONLY GAME WE EVER WON!
WHO DID IT, CHARLIE BROWN? WHO BET ON THE GAME?
YOUR OWN STUPID BABY BROTHER!
RERUN?
RERUN, I'M ASHAMED OF YOU!!
I DIDN'T KNOW IT WAS WRONG... I'M NEW IN THE WORLD!
SCHULZ

RERUN, YOU REALLY LET ME DOWN!
I WAS THE ONE WHO TALKED CHARLIE BROWN INTO LETTING YOU PLAY; SO THEN YOU GO AND GET US INVOLVED IN A BETTING SCANDAL!
I ONLY BET A NICKEL...WHAT ELSE CAN YOU DO WITH A NICKEL THESE DAYS?
OF COURSE, I MUST ADMIT ONE THING...
YOU'RE THE FIRST PERSON WHO EVER HAD THE COURAGE TO BET ON CHARLIE BROWN'S TEAM
I'LL DRINK TO THAT!
SCHULZ

THERE'S ONE THING I STILL DON'T UNDERSTAND..
RERUN BET A NICKEL THAT OUR TEAM WOULD WIN...
WHO DID HE BET WITH?
WHO BET AGAINST US?
SCHULZ

HE'S COMING! HE'S COMING!
THANK YOU, EASTER BEAGLE! THANK YOU!
THANK YOU
THANK YOU VERY MUCH

THANK YOU
THANK YOU!
EVERYBODY GETS AN EGG FROM THE EASTER BEAGLE
WHO DO I GET ONE FROM?
HIS ASSISTANT!

YAWN
Z

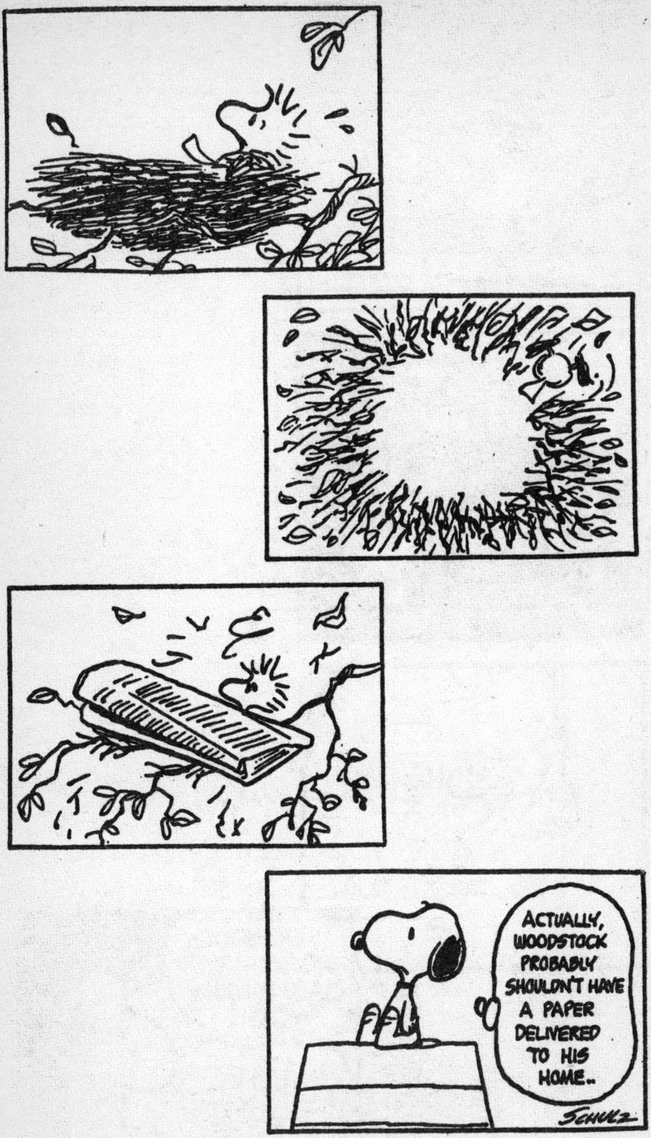
ACTUALLY, WOODSTOCK PROBABLY SHOULDN'T HAVE A PAPER DELIVERED TO HIS HOME..
SCHULZ

WOODSTOCK WOULD HAVE MADE A LOUSY MOTH!
SCHULZ

Kindest regards,
Snoopy
S/w
Dictated but not read.